Rainy Day
Paris

A Practical Guide:

100 Places to Keep Dry

Wendy Lyn

Photography by
Sam A Harris

quadrille

North 32

Central 10

West 56

East 102

South 80

Introduction

The iconic film *Midnight in Paris* sums up this book best with its quote, 'Paris is the most beautiful in the rain'. France's capital has so many things to do on a drizzly day that it really doesn't matter what the weather's doing. Paris is laid out across the left and right banks of the Seine River in a close-knit web of neighbourhoods, called *arrondissements*, which makes the city compact and easy to explore on foot. Each arrondissement has its own distinct feel and demographic; the fashion set gravitates to the west's right bank for luxury shopping and fashion houses around the 'Golden Triangle' avenues, while literature and art enthusiasts meander the galleries along the left bank between the Boulevard St-Germain, Musée d'Orsay and St-Germain-des-Prés church. In Paris' geographical centre, you'll find the Louvre on the right bank with Notre Dame on the island. The star of Paris' skyline, the Eiffel Tower, is on the extreme far west on the left bank, her views changing as the Seine River curves. The hip north, central and east arrondissements on the right bank are more residential, with just a few grand monuments such as Sacré Coeur to the far north. In this book are the neighbourhoods to guide you away from over-touristed sites and into vibrant places with eating, culture and nightlife at their core.

You could start the day at one of Paris' artisan bakeries for buttery *viennoiseries* (croissants, pains au chocolat), before exploring the small galleries tucked away in the charming Marais side streets, with their wide, covered terraces, cafés made for rainy days. However, as charming as the large 24-hour corner places seem, food-focused visitors should know that they serve mostly watered-down coffee and have laminated menus offering quick foods and cheap wine. You are better off going to the small independent spots mentioned in this book for speciality-roasted coffee and fresh hand-baked goods, where you can settle in for hours with a good book or sketchpad.

If you're on the go and want a light bite for lunch, you can eat fantastic street-food sandwiches like a *jambon-beurre* baguette while sheltering under an awning, before keeping dry by shopping in independent bookshops or concept stores. Although these residential areas aren't overrun with visitors queuing for monuments, there is still plenty to see in the smaller museums and cultural venues like the Atelier des Lumières digital art centre, the Musée de la Musique with over 8,000 instruments from the 16th century to today, and the world's most visited cemetery, Père Lachaise. End your day by sipping craft cocktails in a lively cocktail bar before dinner in a modern sharing plates wine bar.

While we're talking about alcohol, 'day drinking' is not common in French culture as most wine and cocktail bars open at 5pm when Parisians are particularly fond of *apéro* hour (short for *apéritif*) as a set part of the day – in fact, it's rarely missed – a time to socialize and wind down as a transition from work to home. These places can be *caves à manger* (wine shops with a license that permits them to open the bottles on the premises but must serve food in the form of bar snacks), where people gather to socialize standing up, or seated in *bars à vins* (wine bars) that function like a restaurant with sharing plates of cold/hot food that must be served with alcohol.

Whatever you are craving, Paris is an exciting, vibrant and diverse eating city with far more on offer after you've had your fill of traditional bistrots. Whether it's bowls of Vietnamese pho, handmade Italian pasta, modern Japanese or French-Chinese fusion, you will not go hungry.

Regardless of whether you picked up this book in Paris while taking shelter in an independent bookshop, or whether you are planning ahead for a visit, I hope these recommendations will reassure you that Paris is truly the most beautiful in the rain.

When to travel

Paris experiences warm summers and cold winters with rainfall all year round. The best time to visit Paris is in the summer with eight hours of daily sunshine, when daytime temperatures are hot and nights relatively warm. It is worth mentioning that most cafés, wine bars and restaurants are not air conditioned and can be stifling indoors with only rotating fans in use for some relief (and also that some smaller establishments close for the full month of August, when many Parisians leave the city).

On average, the coldest months in Paris are January (6.8°C/44.2°F*), February (8.1°C/46.5°F) and December (6.8°C/44.2°F), while the warmest months are June (22.6°C/72.6°F), July (24.6°C/76.2°F) and August (24.8°C/76°F). The city is at its wettest in May (average monthly rainfall is 66mm/2.5in), July (73mm/2.8in) and December (75mm/2.9in). If you're hoping to dodge the downpours, the month with the lowest average rainfall is February (46mm/1.8in).

*All temperatures are the average maximum temperature

Note: All stats are from the Met Office.

About this book

While the 100 recommendations listed in this book offer an insightful look into France's capital, the selections are just a starting point. After more than 20 years of living and working here as a restaurant-hospitality consultant, TV producer and journalist in the food and travel industry, these are the sorts of places I personally recommend to friends, family, first-time visitors and locals living here. In these pages you'll find a mix of unmissable independents, cultural institutions and unique opportunities away from tourist zones, to see neighbourhoods where Parisians live, work and play. This book is designed to be your ultimate roadmap to the neo-bistrots, street food, natural wine bars, sourdough bakeries, craft cocktail bars and fun after-hours hangouts that you might not otherwise have known about. Except for some restaurants, guided visits or exhibitions that need advance tickets, the book does not include any activities which would require much forward planning.

The chapters are divided roughly by geographical area – central, north, west, south and east, with 20 places in each. Although not the geographical centre, I've put the Bastille monument in the 12th on the right bank as the focal point of the Central chapter and worked outwards from there. These neighbourhoods have fewer tourist monuments, making it easy to discover authentic residential areas jam-packed with the four categories: Cafés & Restaurants, Pubs & Bars, Shops and Art & Culture. For an international world capital, Paris is surprisingly compact. Thanks to the snail-shaped outward spiral of the arrondissements, most chapters are easily reached on foot or by bicycle, while accessing others makes more sense using the métro, bus, tram or G7 taxis if it is raining.

To make things as simple as possible throughout these pages, there is a key which includes the following categories:

☺ **Family-friendly** Paris has brilliant things to do with children, from hidden boat canals, dinosaur skeletons in the natural history museum and city museums with clever tours created at their height. It's worth noting that many cultural institutions offer free tickets for children, or discounted family tickets.

✪ **Free** Most of Paris' cultural institutions are free to visit on Sundays and even all-night on the third Saturday in May – the downside, however, is many can pack out on wet days. The best museums and galleries with special events and exhibitions might include a separate entry fee. Check online before you visit.

⊘ No reservations Most Parisian restaurants – even the smallest and most casual – require booking at least two or three weeks in advance. For that reason, this book includes lots of restaurants and wine bars that don't offer reservations at all. At these places, it can be worth getting there early, or later after the first seating. Most venues are happy to put your name down for a table and suggest where to get a drink in the area while you wait. All places accept walk-ins; however, seats are not held back. You can try your luck but do have a backup plan so you have time to try other restaurants.

🖥 Booking ahead recommended As mentioned, while most of the venues in this book don't require a large amount of forward planning to visit, it is worth booking ahead if you can. It is still quite new for small independent restaurants, late-night cocktail bars and wine bars to have online booking systems, so if you have your heart set on a place, don't hesitate to try calling. It also can't hurt to ask to be put on the waitlist if they are fully booked. When it comes to big blockbuster museum exhibitions or concerts, they tend to get booked up in advance.

Getting around

Public transport

The most picturesque way to explore Paris is by walking, but when it's raining the most efficient way to get around is by using the RATP public transportation network which include buses, the métro, the RER and trams. Although the transport system maps will include all three, you will be using the métro for the entries in this book. It's a straightforward system that's easy to navigate, even for first-time visitors. The métro is open from 5.30am to about 1.15am. On Friday and Saturday evenings, as well as on the day before a bank holiday, trains run until about 2.15am. The RER operates daily from 5.30am to about 1.20am.

Head to ratp.fr (there is an English option) for short- and long-term ticket travel pass fees or download the Bonjour RATP app for status updates, maps and journey planning. If you have questions, ask a gate agent before going through the turnstile or the bus driver as you board (the website and app can alert you to any changes or closures). A helpful métro tip when exiting a train car is to consult the neighbourhood map which shows multiple *sorties* (exits) getting you to the closest exit based on your destination.

Cycling

If you've got the proper wet-weather gear, then don't let any showers deter you from getting around Paris by bike. With its segregated cycle lanes, you'll see an abundance of Parisians gliding around the city effortlessly. There are a few bike hire options; one of the biggest is the Vélib' Métropole. Introduced by the City of Paris in July 2007, this large-scale public bike-sharing system now has almost 20,000 bicycles and 1400 docking points in the Greater Paris area. Vélib' Métropole offers electric (blue) and self-service mechanical (green) bikes, so you can easily take your pick. Various passes are available for hire, ranging from 3€ for a one-way 45-minute trip to a 3-day pass for 20€. You can also set up a 12-month subscription to use the service. Go to velib-metropole. fr for subscriptions, maps and a handy 5-minute tutorial called 'How it Works'.

Taxis

When it's pouring, nothing beats a dry taxi. However, only get into government-licensed and metered taxis like G7 with the well-known 'Taxi Parisien' lamp on the roof. G7 Taxis is the biggest taxi network in Europe and using the mobile app in English is incredibly easy, where you can pre-book a ride, track your route in real time and can even pay for your ride directly through the app on g7.fr/en/. Another upside to a G7 taxi is that they are able to use the designated bus- and taxi-only lanes, making for fast and zippy transfers if it isn't rush hour. You can hail G7 on the street if the roof lamp is green, or find one at a designated taxi stand, usually at larger intersections or roundabouts. There's also a wealth of non-G7 car apps, including Uber, but without being able to use the designated bus and taxi lanes, the waits for these cars to pick you up and then get you where you are going can be unbearable.

Central

(3rd, 4th)

The right bank's historic Le Marais (or just Marais) is buzzing day and night with vibrant restaurants and popular nightlife spots. Its two districts may be small, but they offer many culinary and cultural opportunities within its borders defined by cobbled streets, pedestrian thoroughfares and 17th-century mansions. The northern Marais (3rd arrondissement) bordering République is where you'll find most locals doing their food shopping along the rue de Bretagne and Marché des Enfants Rouges (the oldest covered food market in Paris), whereas the southern Marais (4th arrondissement) near the Seine River is the LGBTQ+ hub of the city, and where visitors go shopping in small boutiques and the iconic BHV department store.

Bistrot des Tournelles

Tucked away on a tiny street between Bastille and Place des Vosges, Édouard Vermynck's charming bistrot already feels like a long-time favourite, boasting timeless allure behind lace window curtains. Check in at the century-old marble bar before being seated at intimate wooden tables illuminated by candlelight reflected in large, gilded wall mirrors. The menu is a bistrot lover's dream, where each dish tells a story. Indulge in classics like eggs mayo and the comforting Comté & jambon croque-monsieur. Don't miss the *Daube de Boeuf à la Provençale, Steak Frites* (steak and fries) or the buzzworthy *Cordon Bleu* paired with all-you-can-eat frites and dreamy puréed potatoes. Dessert's a tough call too, with options like *Mousse au Chocolat, Madagascar Vanille Crème Brulée* and *Tarte Tatin* (with raw cream and crunchy sea salt bits). Venture into natural wines with Ed, who'll guide you to remarkable bottles from small regional producers with a particular focus on Beaujolais.

6 rue des Tournelles, 4th
bistrotdestournelles.com
@bistrotdestournelles
☺ 🏠

Les Enfants du Marché

Les Enfants du Marché

Who says that fine dining isn't fun? Just follow the music inside the covered Marché des Enfants Rouges (the oldest food market in Paris) and join the queue at Mika Grosman's acclaimed bar-counter: *Les Enfants du Marché* – where just the name alone 'children of the market' sets the playful tone. Dive headfirst into the à la carte menu options built for sharing alongside locals, farmers and wine growers, and international celebrities sporting caps and shades. Don't be misled by the lively beach-party vibes, the quality and presentation are next level. Kick off with bites such as fresh grilled sardines, mussels and tangy gorgonzola cream, pristine red tuna belly, sweet langoustines and caviar, and earthy morel mushrooms in Jura white wine. For heartier options, work your way up to enormous grilled Brittany blue lobster or *côte de boeuf*. Navigating the wine list is a breeze with Mika as your personal guide to the bottles he's sourced directly from small producers. *Les Enfants du Marché* isn't just a meal; it's a spirited gathering of like-minded adventurers who have come together to share an indulgent meal that is *anything* but ordinary.

39 rue du Bretagne, 3rd
@lesenfantsdumarche
☺ ⊘

Carboni's

Italian food is having a real moment right now, with regulars and first-time visitors alike loving *Carboni's* in the Marais. Step inside the velvet curtains of this buzzy corner spot to find a cosy, open dining room filled with lush greenery, comfortable banquettes, terracotta floors and gilded wall mirrors reflecting sun-drenched days or flickering candlelight by night. Everything on the menu is comforting and made from scratch like *Vitello Tonnato*, *Veal Milanese* and *Pici Cacio e Pepe*, paired with an extensive wine selection made up of small independent producers. Book ahead if you can. For solo diners, the bar by the kitchen is a great option. A bonus is being able to go early or stay late for craft cocktails and music in their no-reservation subterranean *Bar Sotto* with vaulted brick ceilings, a Marshall vinyl jukebox or live band (see page 19).

45 rue du Poitou, 3rd
carbonisparis.com
@carbonis.paris
☺

The Butcher of Paris

It's not every day diners can eat lunch and dinner in their local butcher's shop. Arrive hungry at Louis-Marie Martin's meat counter-steakhouse-natural wine bar tucked inside the lively Marché des Enfants Rouges food market. First-timers ambling through the market's produce, fish and cheese aisles feel like they've stumbled upon something special, in-the-know out-of-towners eat here regularly and local characters straight from central casting linger here every Sunday from lunch until dinner time. The owner knows that quality meat starts far before it reaches the plate. He works with only a dozen French ranchers who ensure the quality of the animal's life. Look forward to XXL portions of farm-butter, charcuterie, aged beef, lamb and more paired with bottles of wine sourced as carefully as the meat. It's a no-reservation walk-in situation, good to know as weekdays are more serene than the lively weekends, where tables or even seats at the counter can be tough to snag.

39 rue de Bretagne, 3rd
thebutcherofparis.com
@thebutcherofparis
☺ ⊘

Parcelles

In the heart of the Marais, Sarah Michielsen and Bastien Fidelin have woven magic into every thread of their cosy wine-focused *Parcelles Bistrot* (named for parcel plots of wine vines). The area's medieval essence lingers in every corner – a testimony to the tales etched into leaning stone and timber walls with only a handful of white linen tables. Regulars come often to find the gems on the wine list paired with the menu, walking the line between classic and innovative: lighter-than-air potato gnocchi brushed with sage butter, delicate Guilvinec sole dressed in clam sauce, crispy veal sweetbreads, meaty foie gras and duck pistachio crust *pithivier* 'pies' and more. Don't even think about skipping dessert, the chocolate tart with candied pecans is sinful. You'll feel so at home here, you'll lose track of time. The only good thing about leaving is the walk home on narrow pavements under the warm glow of historic yellow lamps.

13 rue Chapon, 3rd
parcelles-paris.en
@parcelle_paris

Parcelles

Candelaria

Stop at the pink neon 'tacos' sign in the window of this miniscule brightly coloured hotspot and you've found one of the top mezcal taqueria bars in the world. It is exactly what you'd expect from an authentic taqueria, with homemade guacamole, slow-cooked pork tacos, frozen margaritas and a welcoming vibe. But there's a bonus hidden from view via a discreet door in the kitchen. In complete contrast to the front, you'll find their agave-based cocktail bar is a sexy candlelit lounge with pillows scattered on comfortable seating around low tables. The friendly and knowledgeable bartenders – including guest mixologists from around the world – create seasonal-thematic drinks (non-alcoholic versions as well), and although the list changes often, you'll always find the *La Guepe Verte* (agave with jalapeño and cucumber). They also have a sister cocktail/wine bar in the same area, *Le Mary Celeste* (see page 20).

52 rue de Saintonge, 3rd
candelaria-paris.com
@candelariaparis

Little Red Door

This cosmopolitan spot in the heart of the Marais has been in the prestigious World's 50 Best Bars list ten times, recently listed as #6. However, the little red door doesn't open, it's just to let you know you're in the right location. Step inside the left entrance into this walk-in only, quirky Alice in Wonderland universe of cocktails and flavours. With low lighting and exposed brick walls, it's the perfect intimate place to catch up with friends – especially those who appreciate serious drinks with a side of fun. Bartenders can make what you wish, but they get the most enjoyment from having you guess the ingredients after choosing from the illustrated menu with only the drink's name listed. For small groups, it's possible to reserve seats for guided cocktail flights.

60 rue Charlot, 3rd
lrdparis.com
@littlereddoorparis

The Cambridge Public House

Somewhere between a cosy English village tavern and a trendy Soho cocktail bar, this warm and friendly 'cocktail-pub' is a favourite staple in the Marais. Run by three young lads who have strong backgrounds in the industry, their *Cambridge Public House* consistently wins awards as one of the best bars in the world. True to a British public house, it is a popular gathering spot to meet up with friends at the dark wood bar or sink into a buttery leather sofa in one of the living room-inspired arrangements. Beers, wine and clever craft drinks are on offer with posh pub grub snacks like cheese pasties, meat pies and the legendary sausage rolls. The seasonal cocktails keep things interesting as they are described simply with three descriptive words: 'Nutty - Sustainable - Clarified' is made up of peanut, toasted bread, *flor de caña 12* and *amer du viaduc,* while the 'Fordsmidable - Vegetal - Highball' has celery and jasmine, Fords Gin, Helsinki Akvavit and fizz. Book in advance for spots at the bar; upbeat playlists and bartenders are all part of the vibe.

8 rue de Poitou, 3ʳᵈ
thecambridge.paris
@thecambridge_paris
⊘

Bar Sotto

Carboni's restaurant in the Marais (see page 15) has an unexpected open-to-everyone no-reservations bonus hidden underneath. Follow the stone staircase in front of the bar down to their cosy 20-seat speakeasy for Italian-inspired bar snacks, craft cocktails and great tunes. Whether playing a choice of 45-rpm soul and funk records on their Marshall vinyl jukebox or chillin' to a live jazz band, join those in the know to sip vintage drinks around dimly lit tables on velvet benches until the small hours. The intimate cavern may be small, but the amplified acoustics under the historic brick vaulted ceilings bring the place to life. The drinks and small plates are fun, like the buffalo ricotta with anchovies with a classic Martini or clever Negroni Sbagliato.

45 rue de Poitou, 3ʳᵈ
carbonisparis.com
@barsotto
⊘

Le Mary Celeste

Little sister of the *Candelaria* taqueria bar (see page 18), *Le Mary Celeste* is named after the mysterious 19th-century merchant 'ghost' ship that left New York Harbour for Genoa in November 1872. It was found adrift off the Azores weeks later with no crew onboard – all the alcohol accounted for. This easy-going Marais institution specializes in fresh oysters and craft cocktails shucked and shaken behind the hexagon bar. Hungry groups of friends can gather around wooden tables for platters of raw oysters with *nam jim* sauce and choose from seasonal à la carte sharing plates. Although the menu changes often, regular hits include the soy-marinated devilled eggs, kimchi and cheese fried wontons, Asian/South American-style *ceviche* or the (weekend lunch only) super spicy Korean fried chicken. Walk-ins are welcome, but reservations are strongly advised, especially on weekends when they are open all day from boozy brunches until late dinners. Craft beers, ciders and natural wines are staples, but the staff hold weekly tastings to come up with new creations for the ever-changing list.

1 rue Commines, 3rd
lemaryceleste.com
@lemaryceleste
⊘

Jacques Genin

Jacques Genin is an undisputed cocoa genius; many consider his chocolate the best in the world. Every single piece is made by hand in his workshop or 'lab' without additives, preservatives, flavourings or flavour enhancers. Only pure natural ingredients with as little sugar as possible, as sourced for ganache, praline, fruit jellies, marshmallows, caramels and nougat. You can taste the quality with superb ingredients like fresh Normandy butter, Bronte pistachios and Tahitian vanilla. The modern space with clean lines was purposefully designed around a historic home and its rose garden – leaving the original iron, natural stone, wood beams and chipped plaster in plain view inside the boutique. During festive holiday periods, the frangipane-chocolate galettes and XXL Paris-Brest pastries are in high demand.

133 rue de Turenne, 3rd
jacquesgenin.fr
@jacquesgenin

Sain Boulangerie

Start your day right at artisanal baker Anthony Courteille's beloved shop, where everything is handmade on-site using ancient low-gluten cereal grains resurrected by small French producers. SAIN (meaning healthy) is an acronym for *Saveurs d'Antan Ingrédients Naturels* (Natural Flavours and Ingredients of Yesteryear) and you won't find the sad practice of mass-produced frozen products baked on-site here. Using only ancient wheat, natural yeast that Anthony makes himself and long fermentation times, the result is a healthy bread with a crunchy crust, toast and honey aromas, and an airy and soft crumb. Order crispy, buttery puff pastry like croissants or three-stick pain au chocolat, fragrant breads, fondant cakes, savoury tarts and sandwiches. Purchase items for takeaway or eat in the bright salon where you can see a brigade of people working in the kitchen. Seasonal treats not to be missed are chestnut bread with dried fruits, warm chocolate and ginger brioche, and cinnamon and cardamom rolls.

23 rue des Gravilliers, 3rd
Other location: 13 rue Alibert, 10th
sain-boulangerie.com
@sain_boulangerie
 ☺ ⊘

Fringe Coffee Paris

Single origin coffee, food and photography are the heart of enthusiast Jeff Hargrove's refined pocket-sized espresso bar and shop. Jeff is a long-time photographer who found a delicious way to combine his passions. Whether it is cappuccinos, flat whites or lattes, he works with quality roasters, such as Frukt in Finland. All baked goods are healthy and made in-house, like the Scandinavian-inspired cinnamon and cardamom rolls, chocolate hazelnut cookies with a touch of salt, healthy granola, gluten-free lemon almond cake or soft vegan chocolate banana bread, made using organic flour, eggs and milk sourced from local farmers. An eclectic clientele come to watch the world go by from the benches outside or to check out the rotating selection of photography books, magazines, exhibits and popular vintage sales throughout the year.

106 rue de Turenne, 3rd
fringecoffeeparis.com
@fringecoffeeparis

Merci

Just off a busy boulevard inside a stone courtyard, *Merci* marks its entrance with a red Mini Cooper. It is entirely too easy to spend a rainy day at this former wallpaper factory's eclectic home and lifestyle concept store. You'll find new, cool and what you didn't know you needed under one roof, spread out over three floors. The clever inventory rotates constantly with must-have contemporary items in interior design, gardening, kitchen, stationery, bedroom linens, jewellery and fashion. The star of the show is the one-of-a-kind basement kitchen shop filled with everything to turn any kitchen and dining room into a French dream with cutlery, glasses, themed tableware, hand-crafted wooden spoons, crafted table linens, tea towels, whimsical ceramic cream-puff condiment boxes, hand-forged culinary knives, crockery, covered butter dishes, cookbooks and more. Take a shopping break with a coffee and pastry break at the *The Used Book Café*, reading from one of the 10,000 books.

111 blvd Beaumarchais, 3rd
merci-merci.com
@merciparis
☺ ⊘

Caractère de Cochon

This sliver of a shop is dedicated to ham, where the owner has curated both cooked and aged versions from France, Italy and Spain. Just inside the entrance, he'll help you choose from over 50 varieties on display in his refrigerated case or from the cured dried sausage links, canned pâtés, aged cheese, pickles, butter and the like to build your own baguette sandwich. During the day, locals and visitors stop in to have bread sliced in half and slathered in butter before stuffing it with ham either plain, smoked or flavoured with pepper, truffle, herbs and more. In cold winter months, the neighbourhood lines up for his homemade Alsatian sauerkraut stew with smoky Montbéliard sausage served directly from the piping hot cauldron on the doorstep.

42 rue Charlot, 3rd

@caracteredecochonparis

Musée Carnavalet

Not only is this the oldest museum in Paris, but its purpose is also to present the entire story of Paris from pre-history to today. Housed in the 16th- and 17th-century private mansions the Marais is known for, the *Carnavalet* has over 600,000 historical items such as paintings, sculptures, scale models, coins, photographs, interior decorations and furniture. It's a captivating journey from a Neolithic 2800 BC canoe and Middle Ages and French Revolution artefacts, to what was in Napoleon's luggage and intellectual café life in St Germain des Prés. The favourite exhibit for everyone is in the first rooms, where you can walk through reconstructed Paris street scenes from a century ago. Walk beneath their trade 'signs', when metal images denoted the shop-fronts of pharmacies, restaurants and bakeries, before street numbers and street names were introduced. A charming touch is the routes designed especially for children with kid-sized works and easy explanations just for them. The museum's permanent collections are free and open access, without reservation, but guided and group tours need to be reserved in advance.

23 rue de Sévigné, 3rd
carnavalet.paris.fr/en
@museecarnavalet

Notre Dame Cathédrale

Whether you are a Parisian or a first-time visitor to the capital, gazing up at this imposing 12th-century artistic and spiritual icon will always feel special. Since the tragic blaze in 2019 that ripped through its roof and spire, it has been closed, while the renowned architect Philippe Villeneuve rebuilds the cathedral exactly as it was. Although it is not possible to go inside, it can be admired from the outside – most romantically under an umbrella in rainy weather or via a river boat's glass ceiling. The best viewing point is from behind, on the pedestrian only Pont au Double bridge connecting Notre Dame Park across the Seine River to the left bank. Take refuge underneath the *parvis* (square) in front of the cathedral to see the restoration exhibit in the Archaeological Crypt Museum, which contains fascinating architectural 'city' remains from the Roman town of Lutetia, the origins of Paris.

6 Parvis Notre-Dame –
Place Jean-Paul II, 4th
notredamedeparis.fr
@notredamedeparis
☺ 🏛

Place des Vosges

Originally created as the 'Place Royale' to celebrate the engagement of Louis XIII and Anne of Austria in 1612, the site was renamed 'Place des Vosges' during the French Revolution. Today the park and its surrounding 28 connected private mansions (constructed in the 16th and 17th centuries) is a hidden treasure, literally the backyard to Parisian residents year-round. Situated on the dividing line between the lower (4th arr) and upper (3rd arr) Marais, the *Place* is one of the oldest and most beautiful parks in Paris – even in inclement weather. Stroll under its stunning brick-vaulted arcades to pass time and people-watch at unique shops, art galleries and cafés like *Carette,* most popular on Sundays when the rest of Paris is closed. Its royal past is still reflected in the 5-star *Pavillon de la Reine* hotel and Michelin restaurant *L'Ambroisie.* The most interesting way to approach it is via the southwest entrance on the busy rue Saint-Antoine (#62) where pedestrians step through the carved stone doorways and manicured box-wood gardens of the *Hôtel de Sully,* now headquarters of the *Centre des Monuments Nationaux* (Centre of National Monuments).

62 rue Saint-Antoine, 4th

Fondation Henri Cartier-Bresson

This soaring three-storey building with floor-to-ceiling glass, houses the non-profit Fondation Henri Cartier-Bresson. Both an art gallery and internationally respected organization, it is dedicated to the preservation of one-time power-couple, photojournalists and photographers Henri Cartier-Bresson and Martine Franck. It is proud to share their work, but also host the work of other contemporary photographers, painters, sculptors and illustrators with three different exhibitions a year. Every two years, the HCB prize is awarded to one experienced photographer who has already carried out a significant exhibition in a gallery, museum, publishing house etc. to continue their work. This winner receives €35,000 to carry out another ambitious project with the full backing of the foundation – including international media promotion and recognition.

79 rue des Archives, 3rd
henricartierbresson.org
@fondationhcb

Musée National Picasso-Paris

Located in the heart of the Marais district, known for its sumptuous 17th-century mansions, the former Hôtel Salé is now known as the Picasso National Museum – the world's richest public collection on Picasso. Painted, drawn, sculpted or engraved, over 5,000 works of art in 37 exhibition rooms spread over five floors, they depict Picasso throughout his varied and creative life. Take advantage of guided tours through his blue and pink periods, cubism, surrealism, Spanish occupation and Mediterranean years, though perhaps the most fascinating is the painter's personal collection with great names like Matisse, Derain and Rousseau. Advance tickets can be purchased online and entry is free to anyone under 18 years old. Take a break with a light bite and drink in the café.

5 rue de Thorigny, 3rd
museepicassoparis.fr/en
@museepicassoparis

North

With beautiful Belle-Époque cafés, edgy cocktail bars, eclectic eateries and music venues, there's no shortage of things to do in the Pigalle 9th, Saint-Martin 10th and Montmartre 18th arrondissements. But thanks to the two major train stations bringing visitors in from across the Channel and Charles de Gaulle airport being in the heart of the city, many travellers miss out on the north. Pigalle is the king of nightlife, with award-winning bars, clubs and musical instrument shops reminiscent of its glam-rock-era roots. To the east in the 10th, you'll find diverse street-food venues with an Afro-Caribbean influence especially between the Strasbourg Saint-Denis and Poissonnière metro stations. The 10th is also home to the picturesque 4.6km-long boat canal where its intersection with rue de Lancry is packed with popular wine bars. Far more than just the touristed Sacré Coeur Basilica, the eastern side hilltop village of Montmartre in the 18th has flowering apartment balconies and winding cobblestone streets with sweeping views down across the river, particularly at sunset.

Les Arlots

Just south of Montmartre, Thomas Brachet and sommelier Tristan Renoux's neighbourhood bistrot by the Gare du Nord is a beloved local institution. A soundtrack of joyful noise spills out onto the street as soon as the door swings open, with regulars engaged in animated conversation, corks being pried from bottles and plenty of *santé* (to your health) toasts. Tables are compacted tightly in the small space, with tons of natural light during the day and an intimate atmosphere by night. Unquestionably, the star of the show is their grilled sausage on a bed of puréed potatoes drizzled in meat *jus*, followed by other French classics on the hand-written menu, such as eggs mayo, house-made terrine, steak and seasonal game meat, such as rabbit. Save room for dessert – especially if the rice pudding and salted butter caramel is on the menu. Every single wine bottle is natural and low-intervention, and Tristan is on hand to offer advice on his 250+ references. Les Arlots has a sister wine bar next door, Billili (see page 40).

136 rue du Faubourg Poissonnière, 10th

@lesarlots

Early June

Early June

Owners Victor Vautier and Camille Machet's genius idea? Create an intimate dinner party vibe in a minimalist dining room, give guest chefs from all over the world *carte blanche* to create seasonal sharing plates for a short period of time in the open kitchen, pour natural wines, put on great tunes and open the door on a walk-in basis, unless your group is for more than four people, in which case you have to make a reservation. The result? A runaway hit. Before opening the doors at 6pm, a line has already formed. The vibe is buzzing with locals who know each other – including those that already know the guest chefs. On the plate? It depends. Each chef brings knowledge from their country and experience with inspiration from the local markets. Smaller groups should arrive early or go late for a chance at the handful of seats. Willing to wait? Put your name down and have a drink in the area before they call you to say that your place is ready.

19 rue Jean Poulmarch, 10th
early-june.fr
@earlyjuneparis
⊘ 🗄 (for groups larger than four)

Chantoiseau

This little restaurant is a family affair, run by two young brothers with serious experience working at neo-bistrot *Le Servan* and Michelin-starred *Pierre Gagnaire*. Named after Mathurin Roze de Chantoiseau, the man who opened the first modern restaurant in 1765 near the Louvre with individual tables and dishes to choose from on a menu (these days it's hard to imagine this as a new concept). Nicolas and Julien's modern French classics in a friendly casual atmosphere is a neighbourhood favourite for locals to linger over meals for hours year-round, either outdoors on the terrace or indoors by candlelight.

63 rue Lepic, 18th
chantoiseau-paris.fr
@chantoiseau.restaurant
🗄

Sur Mer

If it weren't for the couples on the narrow terrace sharing oyster platters, even in the rain, you might walk past Olive Davoux's magical little spot and miss it. One peek inside reveals an equally intimate room with regulars tucked in at bar seats on the open kitchen and around a handful of tables. *Sur Mer* means 'on the sea' – because everything is sourced direct from French fishermen, farmers, foragers and winegrowers, all year round, respecting the seasons. Their regional provenance is extraordinary with mussels from Noirmoutier, Camargue clams, Utah Beach oysters, sardines from Saint-Guénolé, tuna from Saint-Jean-de-Luz and Mont-Saint-Michel whelks. Condiments inspired from her travels in South-East Asia are a revelation such as gochujang mayonnaise, nori seaweed, *nam jim* sauce, homemade teriyaki, tangy-sour fermented tofu cream, bright limequat and citrusy ground timut pepper. Reservations are essential.

53 rue de Lancry, 10th
surmer.restaurant
@surmer.paris

Restaurant Cuisine

With its minimalist 70s retro décor, low prices, friendly atmosphere, inventive French-Japanese cuisine and seriously good wines, *Restaurant Cuisine* is textbook neo-bistrot. Since the two young owners have serious food and wine chops between them, having worked in the three iconic neo-bistrots responsible for unpretentious service and natural wines before it was cool (*Chateaubriand, Septime, Le Verre Volé*), it's no wonder they had a devoted following before starting the restaurant. Purposefully unfussy, their brilliant spot on the south side of Montmartre is a must for visiting food and wine lovers. Reservations are essential to enjoy the likes of steamed pork and shrimp ravioli, Galician sea urchins, karaage-style pigeon, dong po braised pork belly with white rice, egg, bok choy, and shiitake... with vegan options such as tofu, sweet padrón pepper, shiitake, grated *daikon* (winter radish) and *dashi* (Japanese soup stock) broth.

50 rue Condorcet, 9th
restaurantcuisine.fr
@restaurant_cuisine

Café les Deux Gares

Finding a great place to pass rainy hours waiting for the Eurostar is no longer a challenge. Literally sitting between two of Paris' busiest train stations (Gare du Nord, Gare de L'Est), this corner spot is a retro throwback to the area cafés that once met the needs of travellers around the clock. These cafés were open at dawn for croissants and espressos at the bar (often with a cheeky glass) followed throughout the day with non-stop service for affordable bistrot meals into a late-night snack, until the last Pullman left the station. Whether it's coffee or wine, their covered terrace is the best place to people-watch with drinks. If you happen to miss the train, it is the perfect excuse to stay at the adjoining *Hôtel Les Deux Gares* with breath-taking city views and to try chef and part-owner Jonathan Schweizer's deeply delicious à la carte/set menus for lunch or dinner.

1 rue des Deux Gares, 10th
@cafelesdeuxgares
 ☺

Sister Midnight

At *Sister Midnight*, the motto is 'our favourite time of day is night' and they mean it. Named after the hit song by Iggy Pop and David Bowie, this award-winning craft cocktail bar is proud of its friendly weekend drag and burlesque performances – all reminiscent of Pigalle's forgotten glam rock roots. The décor is 1970s Berlin fabulous, too, with its teal blue textured walls, velvet curtains, faux leopard, mirrored ceilings and disco balls swirling in rhythm to the likes of The Cramps and Talking Heads. Take a seat at the bar or settle into banquettes for the British finger food and cheese plates to soak up cocktails like house favourites Strawberry Field Forever (gin, aquavit, Dolin bitters, lemon, red pepper and strawberry), Goo Goo Muck (gin, peach soju, Thai basil, lemon, kefir, all with clarified milk) or a tap cocktail such as the sparkling Sister Midnight (vodka, jasmine syrup, cardamom, star anise and lemon).

4 rue Viollet-le-Duc, 9th
sistermidnightparis.com
@sistermidnightparis
⊘ (for bar) and 🍴 (for weekend shows)

Billili

While first-time visitors make their way to find it, locals know the way by heart. Within walking distance from the Gare du Nord, this ultra-cool natural wine bar is a hybrid of the co-owners' children's first names. They created *Billili* hot on the heels of their uber-successful *Les Arlots* bistrot next door (see page 34). Friendly staff and killer playlists keep everybody singing, glasses clinking and the good times flowing. Grab one of the kitchen bar seats or gather with friends around a low table for hot and cold snacking plates and plenty of wine. Don't miss the charcuterie, house *pâté en croute*, oysters, croquettes with béarnaise, *onglet* (hanger steak) tartare, classic egg mayo, confit pork belly and mustard, cheese, and more.

136 rue du Faubourg Poissonnière, 10ᵗʰ
@Billili

Lolo Cave à Manger

Lolo Cave à Manger

Count on a party atmosphere at this popular no-reservation natural wine bar, where a young crowd spills out on the pavement until late night. The social vibe doesn't mean they don't take their food and wine seriously though. It is a hub for visiting chefs who make guest appearances turning out sexy tapas-style plates like handmade potato chips with raw cream and caviar, grilled duck heart skewers, fried chicken or slow-cooked BBQ pork shoulder. Although there are tables, mostly everyone eats standing up. A pro-tip is to start here for apéro and snacks before going to Lolo's bistrot around the corner or have dinner at the bistrot first, then make your way here for some dancing after midnight. It can get so crowded that the windows fog up, reducing their red 'lolo' neon sign to a mere glow.

12 rue de Châteaudun, 9th
lolocaveamanger.fr
@lolocaveamanger

Chop Chop Love

Ismaël's and Ramy's unassuming natural wine bar is the real deal. It is the heartbeat of rue du Faubourg Saint-Martin, bringing together a like-minded inclusive community of international culture, music, fashion, arts, and food and wine. Attached to the historic *La Chope des Artistes* bistrot next door, this modern bar represents the melting pot of local characters that make up the fabric of the neighbourhood. Hanging out and camaraderie is raised to an art form here, with residents and other Paris restaurateurs stopping by to catch up with one another over a game of dominoes, a juicy bottle of wine and tapas. With guest chef friends invited to cook, *Chop* is the ultimate place to meet chefs from other parts of the world and to discover small independent wine producers (who also drop in). From apéritif to late night, it's a refreshing chance to slow down and share time together.

48 rue du Faubourg Saint-Martin, 10th
@chopchop.love

Clove Coffee

Although this welcoming neighbourhood shop is at the crowded foot of Sacré Coeur, it is a rare gem. Locals, neighbours and tourists alike are taking a much-needed coffee break with ethically sourced beans from The Picky Chemist, Dak Coffee Roasters, Manhattan Coffee Roasters, Passenger Coffee from Lancaster, Pennsylvania and even Artéfact teas. The calm, minimalist space is an ideal refuge from the chaos outside – warmed by brick walls, speciality coffee aromas and freshly baked treats like fragrant fresh-out-of-the-oven cardamom rolls from Leonie Bakery. The owners take pride in their precision coffee using custom filtration systems and espresso baskets for clear, expressive and balanced extraction. Co-owner Fatima makes all the pottery for the cups which correspond to specific coffee orders for double espressos, flat whites and/or filtered coffee etc.

14 rue Chappe, 18th
@clovecoffeeshop
 ☺ ⊘

Ozlem Doner

Everyone from local chefs to international media are lining up for the ultimate döner kebab sandwich at Edip's Turkish neighbourhood restaurant, started by his father in 1987. In the heart of Saint Denis, this is a Parisian favourite for the quality of the food as much as the owner, because you'll find him chatting with the customers at the tables every single day. He believes that quality takes time. Whether for sandwiches or plates, the veal, lamb, turkey and chicken are marinated for hours before being roasted, then carefully cut and stuffed inside lighter-than-air homemade bread with red onions, parsley and sumac. The *lahmacun* – rolled pancakes decked out with tender chopped beef and veal, tomatoes and onions – are incredible. Pro tip: the lines can get long, so pre-order by phone before you go.

57 rue des Petites Écuries, 10th
@ozlem_doner
⊘

Dumbo

Pun intended, Dumbo (named after the Brooklyn area called DUMBO – Down Under the Manhattan Bridge Overpass) was a smashing success the minute they opened their first location in Pigalle, consistently ranked one of the best smash burgers in Paris. Owners Charles Ganem and Samuel Nataf recently launched the next branch of griddled patty love on the east side of the trendy rue des Petites Écuries. With its beautiful cream façade and gleaming white counter, regulars line up non-stop for the responsibly sourced dry-aged beef stacked on a potato bun, house pickles, American cheese, onions, mustard and ketchup then 'smashed' on a hot grill. Also on the menu is a vegan version and, if not sold out, a juicy buttermilk fried chicken burger. Their *frites* are so nice they fry them twice.

14 rue des Petites Écuries, 10th
Other location: 64 rue Jean Baptiste, Pigalle, 9th
dumboparis.com/menu
@dumboparis
☺ ⊘

The French Bastards

Today, there is no shortage of great bakeries in Paris but, up until recently, it was the norm for more than 90% of them to use industrial ingredients with quantity over quality as a rule. Not so at *The French Bastards*, a playful nickname for the good-natured owners Julien, David and Manu. They are part of an early wave of young, next generation bakers sourcing ancient grains, organic rye flours and natural yeasts combined with long fermentation techniques to create fantastic rustic breads, *viennoiseries* (croissants, pains au chocolat, etc.) and stunning dessert pastries they call *foodporn*. Their beautiful products contain fresh butter, seasonal fruits, nuts, and Valrhona chocolate. If you are waiting in line, make sure to look for the team working in the pastry kitchen to the likes of Led Zeppelin, rolling out delicious treats with a *Whole Lotta Love*.

65 rue Jean-Baptiste Pigalle, 9th
Other location: 61 rue Oberkampf, 11th is a favourite,
for more locations see website
thefrenchbastards.fr
@the_french_bastards
☺ ⊘

Taka et Vermo Artisans Fromagers

Even though the busy rue du Faubourg Saint-Denis has dozens of food boutiques, this modern *fromagerie* is the only cheese shop. Taking its name from the first syllables of the two young owners' last names, Laure Takahashi and Mathieu Vermorel both honed their craft in other top *fromageries* before crowdfunding to open their own place. Today, it is a cherished venue among residents, wine bars and restaurants who count on its extraordinary raw milk and aged cheeses. Each one is made with traditional methods from artisanal producers before being stored in the underground *affinage* (ripening and ageing) *cave*. In addition to classic Comtés and creamy *bleus*, they have creative ideas throughout the seasons combining cheese with wild plants, spices, fruits and vegetables such as the fresh goat's cheese topped with yuzu confit and lime zest, Brie with walnuts or Saint-Nectaire with sansho pepper.

61 bis rue du Faubourg Saint-Denis, 10th
Other location: 20 rue des Gravilliers, 3rd
takavermo.fr
@takavermocheeseshop

Canal Saint Martin Boat Cruise

Even in inclement weather, this covered boat cruise is an ideal way to see a part of Paris most visitors never see. For Parisians and visitors alike, it's a real treat to sit back and watch tranquil neighbourhoods pass by in slow motion from the Canal Saint Martin. Napoleon Bonaparte originally ordered the construction of the canal to connect Paris with food and goods from other regions, but his nephew's engineer, Baron Haussman, needed to create a broad new boulevard along the same route. He cleverly pushed the canal underground from the Place de la Bastille, where you'll pass through four locks and two swing bridges to Parc de la Villette. Departure points include the Port de l'Arsenal (pedestrian access opposite 50 boulevard de la Bastille) in the 12th, and Bassin de la Villette (opposite 13 quai de la Loire), in the 19th. Along the way, you'll pass many lovely cafés, bars and restaurants in the 10th (many of them in this book).

@Canauxrama

canauxrama.com

 ☺

Folies Bergère

The *Théâtre des Folies Bergère* is one of the most famous theatres in the world. Originally built as an opera house in 1869, two decades later it transformed into the first music-hall review show of the 19th century featuring extravagant costumes and sets. When Josephine Baker caused a sensation dancing only in a banana skirt, the *Folies Bergère* cemented its status in French culture. Additionally, Édouard Manet's famous painting 'A Bar at the Folies-Bergère' (in the Courtauld Gallery, London) is based on a barmaid named Suzon who worked there in the 1880s. Everyone from Edith Piaf and Ella Fitzgerald to Dalida, Chaplin and Sinatra have appeared on stage. Take a private tour behind the scenes backstage or book into a show. Cameras are prohibited.

32 rue Richer, 9th
foliesbergere.com
@foliesbergere_officiel
🖰

Musée National Gustave Moreau

When the undisputed master of French Symbolism Gustave Moreau died in 1898, he donated his magnificent three-storey house, paintings and drawings to France. As the son of a wealthy family born with poor health, his parents encouraged him to draw from an early age. Eventually, his father secured a job for him as a copyist at the Louvre, where he was mentored by artists like Henri Matisse, counted Théodore Chassériau and Edgar Degas as friends and was an inspiration to the early surrealists like Dalí. What set him apart from other artists is that his wealth and talent gave him the freedom to create what he wanted, without needing public showings or benefactor sponsorship. Because of this, he led a reclusive lifestyle and not many of his works ever left this house, so to see Moreau's work today is a rare opportunity.

14 rue Catherine de la Rochefoucauld, 9th
musee-moreau.fr/en
@museegustavemoreau

L'Olympia

After opening in 1893, this historic building went through more than a century's worth of unsuccessful ventures (horse track, amusement park, circus and cinema, to name a few), plus renovations, transfers of ownership, legal battles and near bankruptcies. It finally became a landmark music venue in the 1950s when the exterior façade of the venue was redone in red neon lights announcing the names of the artists in capital letters, notably the octagon 'O' shape mirroring the aerial view of Paris' ring road. Notable performers were Edith Piaf and even the Beatles, who played three shows a day from January to February 1964, when 'I Want to Hold Your Hand' reached number one in America. Since then, legendary performers such as the Grateful Dead, Sting, Jimmy Hendrix, The Rolling Stones, Madonna, Led Zeppelin and even Taylor Swift have graced the historic theatre. Today it is one of the hottest rock venues a band can hope to play, especially seeing 'their' names in the famous lights. Any music fan would be thrilled to take in a show at *L'Olympia*.

28 blvd des Capucines, 9th
olympiahall.com
@olympiahall
 ☺

Palais Garnier

Often referred to as 'the wedding cake', Charles Garnier's masterpiece built for Napoleon III is one of the most beautiful opera houses in the world, especially on a rainy day. Its ornate Chagall chandelier and globe candelabras cast a warm golden glow over the winding staircase and elaborate marble foyers – a peaceful refuge from the mad traffic circle out front in inclement weather. *The Palais Garnier* inspired Gaston Leroux's novel *The Phantom of the Opera,* which in turn inspired the award-winning musical hit, written by Andrew Lloyd Webber. There is a fascinating tour at 5pm that takes place after the opera has closed to the public, when visitors have the building to themselves. Guides take you backstage to see the inner workings of the sets, to dressing room number 5 and answer fans' questions about whether there's really an underground lake (the answer is yes) and if the chandelier scene was based on a true event (again, yes, when in 1896 a steel cable detached during a performance, killing one person and injuring many).

Pl. de l'Opéra, 9th
operadeparis.fr/en
@operadeparis
☺ 🏛

West

In the mood to go disco bowling, take in a movie at an
Art Deco cinema, eat authentic Vietnamese cuisine
or appreciate some vinyl listening bars? Perhaps
craft coffee, swanky cocktails or traditional bistrots
are more your scene. If so, get yourself to west Paris.
You'll find wandering the historic cobblestones of the
1st and 2nd arrondissements mostly intimate, funky
and fun, while moving further west into the 7th, 8th
and 16th becomes residential, high-end and exclusive.
In between, pop into cute cafés and restaurants in
neighbourhoods like Les Halles or splash the cash on
the Place de la Concorde in the Hôtel de Crillon bar.

Cloche Brasserie

This recently restored brasserie has come full circle from its early days in Les Halles, the former market district referred to as 'The Belly of Paris'. Nearly two centuries ago, the food vendors not only sold produce, seafood and meat to Parisians coming from far and wide, but the butchers would barter meat with these neighbouring eateries at dawn to cook hearty breakfasts for them before their long work shifts. Although the new team has kept its old-school look and feel with white tablecloths and antique silverware, it is now buzzing with an energy that this part of town had mostly forgotten. Situated on a busy corner underneath the original *cloche* bell, you'll find that the kitchen team has elevated classics like whole char-grilled *sole meunière* dressed in nori butter, Galician beef steaks with buttery potato purée, macaroni with aged Comté cheese and Jura wine, and a savoury *crêpe suzette* with blood orange and mezcal. Stop in for a long lunch or dinner on a rainy day, as this is a great people-watching spot from any table, especially the terrace under the awning.

1 rue Coq Héron, 1st
cloche-paris.com
@clochecloche cloche
🏛

Café des Ministères

When husband-and-wife team Roxane and Chef Jean Sévègnes' (*L'Ambroisie* and *Ducasse* alum) opened a few years ago, it was just what Paris needed. Their traditional cuisine presented with a modern touch in a small humble bistrot was a hit, especially in a part of town known for its sombre Parliament buildings and expensive mansions. The only downside is that reservations are now hard to get. Start with the glorious egg mayo, savoury black Bigorre pork and chicken liver terrine, snails with bone marrow or the stunning Normandy scallops baked in their shell *à la Parisienne,* with *pommes duchesse* – fluffy puréed potatoes – piped into the shell before the entire dish is baked. Although the menu changes with the seasons, Jean has created dishes so well-liked they cannot be taken off the menu, such as the *choux farci* (stuffed cabbage) and the iconic stacked puff pastry *vol-au-vent* garnished with poultry, sweetbreads, lobster, morel mushrooms and green asparagus. Don't give up on getting a taste; the delicious comfort food is worth your effort.

83 rue de l'Université, 7th
cafedesministeres.fr
@cafedesministeres.paris
▣

L'Ami Jean

In an old-school 1930s setting unchanged by time, people come from all over the world for Stéphane Jégo's classic bistrot near the Eiffel Tower. Its reputation is legendary, but there is zero formality. First-time visitors are perplexed at first by the chaos, with regulars crowded around communal tables tearing into gut-busting portions while the chef is yelling from the open kitchen. But this is *L'Ami Jean*, a den of gluttony curated by one of the most talented, and kindest, chefs in Paris. Stéphane is a leader in the bistronomy movement – meaning, serious cooking doesn't have to mean stuffy dining rooms. The minute you sit down you'll be handed an entire country terrine to serve yourself, then pass to the next table. After that, never miss his cream of Parmesan soup poured from a pitcher over tiny croutons and crumbled bacon, butter-basted sweetbreads with truffles, or wild game when in season. He uses the whole animal and doesn't waste a thing. Leave the smart jacket at home and wear your fat pants. Jégo's mission is to feed you like nobody's business, they won't let you say no to the rice pudding dessert.

27 rue Malar, 7th
lamijean.fr
@ l_ami_jean
▣

Groot

Pithiviers-tourtes are one of France's ultimate winter comfort foods, flaky crimped-edged pastries filled with vegetables or meat and baked. French Top Chef Winner 2023 Hugo Riboulet and his former teammate Albane Auvray recently opened the genius *Groot*, a street-food *pithiviers-tourte* pie bar between Les Halles and Frenchie. Now you can have them year-round with seasonal ingredients in handheld manageable versions without the need for sit-down restaurant reservations. It is tiny, with just a handful of seats and a consistent queue for the full four hours (noon–4pm) it's open. The favourite veggie version is a celery confit with citrus fruits, brown mushrooms, porcini and trumpet mushrooms, smoked garlic cream and Granny Smith apple, while meat lovers are raving about the matured smoked beef with potatoes, Raclette cheese and onion compote, and the all-in-one Landes chicken, free-range pork and veal stuffing, buttered cabbage, brown mushroom duxelle, porcini mushrooms and trumpet mushrooms. If you can't go for lunch, take some home for a fancy apéro or easy dinner with vinegary green salad. If you need several, call ahead.

34 rue Saint Sauveur, 2nd
grootlatourte.com
@grootlatourte

Mắm From Hanoï

No need to cross town to Belleville, now you can slurp authentic flavours in the heart of Paris at Tuyet Ngân Bùi and Tuan Anh Tran Luu's modern *phở* canteen, serving northern Hanoi-style foods based on their childhood. The concise comfort food menu is based around four things: spring rolls, *bo* buns, *phở* soup (a staple of Vietnamese cuisine) and a plate of caramelized pork with egg and rice. Every effort is to make as much as possible in house, while sourcing impeccable fresh meat and vegetables directly from French farmers. Start with pork or vegetarian spring rolls generously stuffed between thin rice sheets or the soft pork, beef or vegetarian *bo* buns accompanied by aromatic herbs. *Phở* bowls are fragrant and delicious from their homemade bone marrow broth, delicate rice noodles and tender slices of beef complemented with coriander, lime and even ginger or lemongrass. Complete your meal with filtered Vietnamese coffee using condensed or coconut milk, juices, and French IPA or Saigon beer. It's extraordinarily popular, so don't chance walking-in and be sure to book ahead online.

39 rue de Cléry, 2nd
mamfromhanoi.com
@mam39paris
☺ 🏠 ✓

Faggio Panoramas

Part wood-fired pizza joint, part wine bar and part vinyl bar, it's a vibe at this little 'Paris pizza joint' inside the historic covered Passage des Panoramas. It comes as no surprise since it is also owned by the popular and much larger *Bambino* vinyl record bar in the 11th. Here, they are open every day, but the real fun is twice a month when they invite their rock-star chef friends to collab with them, like *Septime*, *Haikara Deep-Fried* and *Aux Deux Amis*. The passageway fills up quickly with locals curious to taste their take on handmade Neapolitan-style pizzas, cocktails and socialize over good music. Favourites have been the Chilli (tomato sauce, n'duja, fior di latte, *ito togarashi*, sancho pepper) and the Wagyu (fior di latte, *negi* oil and sancho pepper), as well as *Septime*'s duck Bolognese that sold out hours into a 12-hour event.

16 passage des Panoramas, 2nd
faggioparis.com
@faggio_panoramas
@bambino_paris
☺ ⊘

Hôtel de Crillon – Bar Les Ambassadeurs

When the weather isn't cooperating, but you want to dress up, go all out and treat yourself, there is no better place to find shelter than this glamorous 18th-century style hotel bar on the Place de la Concorde. After an extensive four-year renovation, everything is gleaming from the marble columns to the hand-painted 'sky' ceiling and gold-gilded mirrors reflecting the views outside. The soft light filtering though the tall arched windows is breath-taking even on a rainy day, with the obelisk and Louvre just beyond. If you time it right, there is a piano, bass and drum trio that sets the mood while you peruse drinks prepared by smart mixologists. There are also sommeliers on hand to help you choose from the extensive wine list which has over one hundred listings for Champagne alone (including small growers like Sélosse) – perfect with lobster rolls, black truffle Comté *croque monsieur* sandwiches or the French caviars.

10 pl de la Concorde, 8th
rosewoodhotels.com/fr/hotel-de-crillon
@rosewoodhoteldecrillon

Frenchie Bar à Vins

Chef-owner Greg 'Frenchie' Marchand's lively first-come-first-served wine bar has two mottos that set the tone: 'No great story ever started with a glass of milk' and 'Everything I want to eat... everything'. Tucked away on a narrow street opposite his one Michelin star *Frenchie Restaurant*, the wine bar is hundreds of years old with its half-timbered walls and low ceilings. Diners can either stand at the bar or sit at leather-covered communal tables next to an open kitchen. With the casual seating, extensive sharing plates and affordable wines by the glass, you're guaranteed to meet someone and start that great story. Don't miss their warm mini bacon scones with maple syrup and raw cream, lamb confit tossed with handmade *pappardelle,* the extensive cheese platter and *dulce de leche* banoffee. Like what you are drinking? Head direct to their wine shop next door to take it home with you. Give the driver an address for the neighbouring rue Réaumur, as the street isn't wide enough to accommodate cars.

6 rue du Nil, 2nd
Sister restaurants on the same street:
Frenchie Restaurant, L'Altro
frenchie-bav.com
@frenchieruedunil

Goûte Bar à Vins

On rainy days, the pedestrian-only side streets around the busy rue Montorgueil are the most photographed in Paris, due to the number of brightly coloured umbrella and rubber boot reflections on wet cobblestones. Which makes Louis Goument and Olivier Chalifour's warm and friendly *Goûte* (meaning 'taste') a lovely refuge to sip juicy natural wines, nibble on delicious snacks and people-watch. As long-time sommelier friends working at Michelin-starred *Septime* (see page 107) and *Brutos* before joining forces here, the guys know their wine. Chat with them at the bar where they'll help you choose an affordable bottle from the shelves, charging take-away prices with only an 8€ corkage fee. Tasty bites of Kalamata olives, cheeses, cured sausage, pork and chicken *terrines*, *labneh* dressed in figs and honey vinaigrette, and houmous and roasted pumpkin are wonderful. For groups of friends check out the private *table d'hôte* (host's table) where a late afternoon can turn into an early dinner.

8 rue Mandar, 2ⁿᵈ
@goute.paris
⊘

Goûte Bar à Vins

Montezuma Café

Montezuma Café

For vinyl music and wine enthusiasts, do not miss the chance to visit the unique *Montezuma Café* near the Stock Exchange. Inspired by post-war Japanese cafés, this fantastic audiophile bar and bistrot packs in regulars for stellar sound, delicious food and great drinks. The first thing you'll notice when you open the door is the high-quality sound coming from amped-up equipment in the main dining room and jazz vaulted basement cellar downstairs. Drop in with friends or reserve a cosy table upstairs for tasty sharing plates sent up from the open kitchen that you will see halfway down the stairs en route to the cellar. With over 150 affordable natural wines and craft beer and cocktails to choose from, you will not go thirsty. You can also enjoy DJ sets not by professionals, just music lovers who bring their favourite jazz or soul vinyl to share on Thursday, Friday and Saturday evenings.

15 rue Notre Dame des Victoires, 2nd
montezumacafe.com
@montezuma.cafe

Boneshaker Donuts

Leave it to an American pastry chef in Paris to create a community and lifestyle around seasonal handmade donuts, and 100% plant-based donuts at that. Less than ten years ago, Amanda Bankert bought a little home fryer for a few euros at a yard sale in Montmartre to make small-batch donuts for local coffee shops. That led to the opening of her first donut shop, where lines were forming all day to buy products faster then she could cook a new batch. Today, she has a larger space with seated dining and a dedicated team of pastry chefs making addictive vegan donuts, brownies, cinnamon rolls and coffee every single morning, seven days a week. Although the 'OG' – the original glazed classic – will always be on the menu, Amanda changes recipes with the seasons like the apple pie donut (with apple pie filling), the No Sleep Till Brooklyn (filled with lemon curd, dusted with coconut), a pumpkin cake donut, hazelnut beignet and the ABJ (almond butter glaze, blueberry compote).

86 rue d'Aboukir, 2nd
boneshakerparis.com
@boneshakerparis
☺ ⊘

Télescope Café

Passionate coffee enthusiast Nicolas Clerc built a strong international community over the years at his minimalist café, a calm oasis for elevated brewed coffee, espresso drinks and house-made pastries. Its location near the Palais Royale and Louvre is literally a world away (although only by blocks) from major tourist destinations where expensive sub-par coffees are the norm. This once professional photographer is respected as one of the first to lead the third-wave caffeine revolution in Paris, with thoughtful bean sourcing, storage, proper brewing, roasting, temperature and technique. Don't miss the chance to ask Nicolas about any of the beans' back stories over his lemon cake. Not in a talkative mood? Enjoy one of the French or English newspapers against the backdrop of raindrops jazz.

5 rue Villédo, 1st
@telescopecafe
☺ ⊘

Télescope Café

Tapisserie

What did the Septime group do to follow the success of their two legendary restaurants and wine bar on the rue Charonne in the east of Paris? *Bien sûr*, they opened an artisanal bakery-pastry shop named *Tapisserie* (the first and third letters of pâtisserie are inverted). Shortly after, they announced that Tapisserie was also opening across the river on the left bank near École Militaire. From the minute you open the door, the butter aromas hint at the freshly made *viennoiseries* like croissants, pains au chocolat, choux puff pastries and savoury croissants, *jambon-beurre*. Warm up with hot chocolate or with fantastic espresso. Extraordinarily rare for Paris, coffee with oat milk is an option. If it's sweets you crave, don't miss their *kouign-amann* (a sweet Breton pastry), flan or signature maple syrup tart with whipped cream. From breakfast throughout the day, you can eat there or take treats away with you.

16 av de la Motte-Piquet, 7th
Other location: 65 rue de la Charonne, 11th
tapisserie-patisserie.fr
@tapisserie_patisserie
☺ ⊘

Terroirs d'Avenir

Terroirs d'Avenir

Grab your umbrella and food shopping bag to spend time on this little street north of Les Halles. For first-time visitors, the food shops on the narrow rue du Nil entice with their charm. Yet behind their colourful façades is an extraordinary story of how two business-school friends interested in sustainable agriculture travelled France after graduation, and discovered all but forgotten food varieties along the way. It inspired them to act as suppliers, connecting farming families to the chefs and restaurant tables all over the city – including top chef Gregory Marchand whose Frenchie Group restaurants are also on the same street. It didn't take long before they gave the public the same access by opening a produce grocery, fishmonger, butcher, *fromagerie* and bakery – local heroes putting faces to the names of the farmers, fishermen and small producers who grow or raise animals with care.

3-8 rue du Nil, 2nd
terroirs-avenir.fr
@terroirsdavenir
☺ ⊘

Librairie Galignani

For literary or French cooking enthusiasts, if it's raining out, head direct to the *Librairie* (bookshop) *Galignani* across from the Tuileries Gardens, still owned by the direct descendants of the Venetian Galignani family who used one of the first printing presses in Italy to distribute books back in the 1600s before moving to Paris. Lose yourself among the beautiful hardwood shelves stacked high with English and American literature, the fine arts, biographies, language and travel guides, and rare books dating as far back as the 1930s. You'll find everything from fantasy, crime and science fiction novels to stunning illustrated historic and modern-day French cookbooks. There is even a children's section guaranteed to entertain them for hours. Can't find what you are looking for? Galignani offers specialized searches, internet orders and international shipping anywhere in the world. Throughout the year, they organize book signings and events in the store. You will not leave this extraordinary bookshop empty-handed, that is a guarantee.

224 rue de Rivoli, 1st
galignani.fr
@librairiegalignani
☺ ✪

Grand Rex

Originally built in the early 1930s by a wealthy movie producer, distributor and owner of *L'Olympia* (see page 53), this now landmark Art Deco cinema is a registered historic monument. As the largest cinema in all of Europe with multiple screens, it's the 'grand' auditorium that is the showstopper with 3,000 seats spread across three levels and a 100ft-high 'starry' ceiling. When you see photography flashes and long lines outside behind red velvet ropes, you can bet that there is a high-profile world premiere taking place. You can reserve tickets or even better, book behind-the-scenes tours to visit the off-limits projection room, recording studio and film set and learn more about the Grand Rex's fascinating history. A few interesting facts to know is that the Rex is not only a scale model of Radio City Music Hall in New York City, notable film premieres have been *Pinocchio* in 1946 (the first Disney feature film to be shown there), in 1963 Alfred Hitchcock's *The Birds*, and just recently the award-winning film *Oppenheimer* premiered here.

1 blvd Poissonnière, 2nd
legrandrex.com
@legrandrex
☺ 🏛

Bowling Foch

If a game of billiards, late-night dinner, dancing and bowling are (pun intended) right up your alley, this upscale hotspot located underground next to the Arc de Triomphe is the perfect venue to spend time with family and friends when the weather outside isn't so cheery. Families might prefer the daytime, while adults will prefer the evening when they can hit the dancefloor after the games are over. Just follow the tunnel to Le Duplex, a modern entertainment complex with this slick, 15-lane bowling alley, plus *Le Vogue* restaurant and a nightclub. Anyone under 16 years of age needs to be accompanied by an adult and appropriate dress is required, 'no tracksuits or caps'.

1 av Foch, 16th
@duplexparis
bowling-foch.com, leduplex.com
☺

Bibliothèque Nationale de France (BnF)

Nestled in the heart of Paris by the Louvre-Opéra district, the *BnF* (the National Library of France) may not be one of the biggest institutions, but it is one of the most beautiful, especially the *Salle Ovale* (oval reading room). You'll discover collections in various galleries filled with antiquities, maps, music, coins, manuscripts, artwork and precious objects in unexpected settings. The garden, terrace, bakery café, book shop and *Salle Ovale* all grant free access for visitors, even quiet spaces for teleworking. The one-hour-thirty-minute guided tour of the *BnF* allows you to discover the history and learn about the architecture of the grandiose Baroque gallery and the immense oval reading room. It is best to book tickets in advance online (free for under-26).

5 rue Vivienne, 2nd
bnf.fr/fr/richelieu
@labnf
☺ 🏛 ✦

Fondation Louis Vuitton

Known as the 'glass cloud' or LVF, the *Fondation Louis Vuitton* art and culture museum by architect Frank Gehry is in the Jardin d'Acclimatation of the Bois de Boulogne. The landmark curved glass building hosts both major exhibitions and a permanent collection of modern and contemporary art. Get ahead of your visit to this massive cultural centre by planning your key areas of interest on the Fondation Louis Vuitton app (which has some great exclusive content) or using the interactive guide on the website. Families can enjoy unlimited, skip-the-line access, and there's free entry to children under three years old. Beneath Frank Gehry's 'Fish Lamp' sculpture, Le Frank Restaurant is open daily for lunch, or reservation dinners Friday and Saturday. Visitors must be in possession of a valid Fondation admission ticket to enter both Le Frank Restaurant and the Fondation Bookshop. All tickets indicate an admission time.

8 av du Mahatma Gandhi, Bois de Boulogne, 16th
fondationlouisvuitton.fr/en
@fondationlv
☺ 🏛

Passage des Panoramas

It feels like you are stepping back in time to 1799 when walking through this historical national monument that was literally built for rainy days. Originally part of 150 connected covered passageways where the wealthy could step straight from their carriages, regardless of weather, to shop away from muddy Parisian streets which were yet to have pavements, it is still used daily by locals to cut through busy boulevards and streets. Only a handful of passages remain today, and the Passage des Panoramas is the most lively and vibrant, retaining its original architectural character flooded with natural light from the ornate vaulted iron and glass ceiling, and lined with independent shops and eateries. *Racines* is a must for Simone Tondo's delicious home-cooking, or stop in at the popular *Faggio* (see page 63) for pizza, wine, cocktails and popular bi-monthly Sunday popups.

11 blvd Montmartre, 2nd

@passagedespanoramas

South

(5th, 6th, 12th, 14th)

Although Paris' northeast arrondissements get their fair-share of attention, there are plenty of reasons to visit the 12th before heading south across the river to the 5th, 6th and 14th for incredible restaurants, creative cocktail bars, bakeries, street markets and unusual cultural museums. Grab your umbrella and start in the eclectic residential neighbourhood around Square Trousseau Park and Gare du Lyon train station on the right bank, where railway arches and former wine warehouses are home to cafés and lively wine bars, then metro or walk across to the ancient Latin Quarter with its Medieval remnants along winding cobblestone streets for aged cheeses, bakeries and speciality roasted coffee. Saint Germain's side streets between the Seine River and busy main boulevard are where you'll find locals after work, in tiny tucked-away wine bars before sipping on craft cocktails late into the night.

Restaurant AT
(Atsushi Tanaka)

Eight years after opening his first restaurant near the banks of
the Seine, Chef Atsushi Tanaka finally realized his dream of
winning a Michelin star. With a combined interest in fashion,
house music and skin-contact wines, plus having been trained
by the best chefs in Europe, it is no surprise that he describes
his Japanese-French cooking and presentation as an art form.
Everything from the Nordic minimalist dining room, hand-
crafted cutlery, ceramic tableware and imaginative plating of
each course is a work of art. Expect seasonal tasting menus
to feature delicious dishes such as tender king white crab
with shaved white truffles from Alba, delicate turbot fish and
razor clams dressed in spring green peas and caviar, or morel
mushrooms in a black garlic and meat *jus*. As an advocate for
natural wines that have no additives or chemicals, you'll find
a huge selection of small-production European wines as pure
as his cuisine.

4 rue du Cardinal Lemoine, 5th
atsushitanaka.com
@restaurant_AT

Quinsou

On a tranquil street across from the Ferrandi cooking school, Michelin chef Antonin Bonnet's elegant yet understated *Quinsou* is the go-to splurge for brilliant small plate menus paired with natural wines in the Saint-Germain neighbourhood. The no-frills neo-bistrot features soft lighting, cream stone walls, blonde wood tables, buttery leather banquettes and oversized mirrors. Antonin's motto is 'work hard and be nice to people', which is reflected in his incredible staff, refined cooking and quality dayboat seafood, ethical meat and organic produce. The seasons dictate the set menus, where you can find the likes of marinated *maquereaux* (mackerel) alongside sweet peppers and wasabi-infused sour cream; tender 'blonde' Aquitaine beef on a bed of cauliflower purée with nutmeg, hazelnuts, beef juice infused with kombu and toasted nori; and for dessert, if it's on the menu do not miss the biscuit and cardamom chocolate cream with 'chai' mousse.

33 rue de l'Abbé Grégoire, 6th
quinsourestaurant.fr
@quinsouparis

Chanceux

Just a stone's throw from Notre Dame, Thomas Lehoux (known as one of the founders of third-wave coffee) and Farah Laacher's *Chanceux* is a modern gem on the historic rue Galande with its cobblestone street and remnants of Medieval half-timbered houses. Not to be confused with their successful 11th arrondissement right bank location, this new left bank all-day café is also a hit. Visitors and locals alike come for the freshly roasted speciality coffee brewed with the fancy La Marzocco machine, house juices like rosemary lemonade, and daily handmade sandwiches, such as their legendary bacon and hash brown egg bun or fried-chicken schnitzel with melted Cheddar. Those with a sweet tooth haven't been forgotten – the lemon cake, pumpkin cake with sage and vegan chocolate pastries baked each day are worth a visit on their own.

63 rue Galande, 5th
Other location: 57 rue Saint-Maur, 11th
@chanceux.paris

Passerini

Tuscan-born Giovanni Passerini is one of the most talented and well-liked chefs in the city, with many other successful chefs having passed through his kitchens first. His friendly corner *trattoria* balances both rustic and modern food with a casual and refined vibe – it's also one of the most popular restaurants in Paris. When it is raining out, it is the perfect place to have a long meal with a bottle (or two) from their natural wine list. Lunches are straightforward with starters, pasta and mains (don't miss his mouth-watering *Trippa Alla Romana*, or 'Roman Tripe'), whereas à la carte dinners are a bigger sharing affair with suckling lamb or whole pigeon. Going in groups for dinner is strongly advised. For solo diners, you might be more comfortable at their *Passerina* wine bar across the street (see page 89). They have a pasta shop next door, where you can watch them make fresh pasta in their shop every day, and even buy it to take home with you.

65 rue Traversière, 12th
passerini.paris
@passerini_and_co
☺ 🏠

Le Square Trousseau

Named for the leafy green park with gazebo just opposite between Faubourg Saint-Antoine and the Aligre outdoor food market, this historic all-day café and bistrot is a neighbourhood gem open seven days a week. This now stylish area was once considered the suburbs outside the city limits beyond Bastille. Retaining all its original features and elegance from 1907, from the zinc bar to the ornate fixtures and ceilings, at the wide covered terrace with park views you can see the seasons change and watch the world go by, even when it's raining. The classic French menu reads like a dream with oysters, omelettes, onion soup, *tartare*, *steak frites*, *escargots*, truffle *croque-monsieur*, *foie gras*, duck *magret* and frogs legs. The young couple who own it are hospitality pros and make everyone feel as welcome as if in their home. Rare for Paris, there is a stunning private room for groups of more than 10 people.

1 rue Antoine Vollon, 12th
squaretrousseau.com
@squaretrousseau
☺ 🏠

Cravan

If it's pouring out, what better way to ride it out than with craft cocktails and bar food in a bookstore library? The 'new' *Cravan* building is the last remaining historic building on the boulevard, its original 17th-century features blending in with the urban landscape spread over four levels, starring three cocktail bars featuring *Cravan* founder Franck Audoux's mixology experience (he wrote the book *French Moderne: Cocktails from the Twenties and Thirties With Recipes*), which made for a brilliant partnership with Rizzoli NY. You'll find 'Royal' cocktails made with Champagne, a Mad Collins using gin, ginger and sparkling water, or the Isadora made with tequila and sour cherries, as well as classic drinks like French 75s and Old-Fashioneds, too. Enjoy light bar snacks like the gilda with olives, anchovies and chilli peppers or upgrade with the fancy lobster roll with bisque mayonnaise.

165 blvd St Germain, 6th
cravanparis.com/en
@cravanparis

Passerina

Passerina

When *Passerini* (see page 85), one of the best Italian restaurants in Paris, opened an easy-going natural wine bar across the street, it was always bound to be a social affair packed from open to closing. Justine Priot and Giovanni Passerini's buzzy no-reservation bar has small dishes to share with French and Italian wines, around a mahogany bar where it is impossible not to chat to everyone else. Menus are seasonal with favourites such as fennel salami, veal *tonnato*, *porchetta* ramen, *guanciale* dumplings in duck and tarragon broth and cheese and charcuterie plates. The best part of the experience is an open secret, just before closing the chef circulates asking who wants the *Cacio e Pepe* (Parmesan and pepper) risotto, which no one turns down. Their music playlists ensure a good time and if you are truly lucky, Giovanni brings his guitar to play crowd-pleasing songs such as *I Want to Break Free*, when the entire bar breaks out into song along with him.

44 rue Traversière, 12th
@les_avantcomptoirs
⊘

Chez Nous

Saint Germain has a treasure with this natural wine bar, noted by the five stone face finials over the door that match the 381 versions along the Pont Neuf bridge just next door – 16th-century 'mascaron' faces installed above doorways to scare away evil spirits. Nothing frightening here, this friendly bar named 'our house' is welcoming to all, where you'll want to join the locals at the bar or on the terrace with its old stone walls and intimate lighting. Open every day from apéro, whet your appetite before dinner with a bottle from their deep natural wine list featuring small independent producers who refuse chemicals in their wine-making process. Savoury plates to accompany fantastic Champagnes, like Georges Laval and Vouette & Sorbée, can be charcuterie (don't miss the shaved Black Angus beef) with cheese such as Saint-Nectaire drizzled with honey and toasted nuts, fat green olives, buratta cheese, house gravlax, *terrines* and *tartare*.

10 rue Dauphine, 6th
@chez_nous_paris
⊘

Augustin Marchand d'Vins

Situated between the Seine River and Blvd St Germain, this welcoming little independent natural wine bar on the left bank, noted by its red neon sign, has friendly local vibes, fun wine bottles and delicious food. What makes it special is that it isn't only about wine, it's also about eating, tasting, learning and the gracious enthusiastic host sharing his latest discoveries. Grab a seat on one of the retro bistrot chairs around one of the little round tables for more than just typical charcuterie and cheese plates – *Augustin* sources extraordinary garden vegetables and meats for unforgettable hot dishes like *choux farci* (stuffed cabbage) or the gorgeous miniature baked pumpkins stuffed with *Mont d'Or* cheese covered with fresh black truffles. Don't let the centuries-old wooden beams and stone walls fool you, there is nothing old-fashioned about it. Like what you are drinking or need wine to take home? *Augustin* is also a takeaway bottle shop.

26 rue des Grands-Augustins, 6th
@augustin75006

Prescription Cocktail Club

Stepping inside this ground-breaking cocktail bar is pure theatre, an intimate stage setting with jewel-tone plush velvet curtains and furniture, extravagant fixtures and upholstered walls for sipping speciality drinks late into the night. The young owners, Experimental Cocktail Group, are the early founders of craft cocktails in Paris, if not Europe, nearly 15 years ago when cocktails were watered-down cheap drinks at cafés or exorbitantly expensive five-star hotel bars. You can now find their astonishing hotel-bar projects in Venetian palazzos to English country estates. Intimate by design, imagine a young Dalí, Grace Kelly or Sean Connery settling into one of the living room settings, around low-mirrored sofa tables and fireplaces for good cocktails, good company and good times. You can order classics or their custom *Naked Gaga* with Plymouth Gin, Cocci Americano, Aperol, citron syrup, Bourgoin verjuice and lemon bitters, or *karl* using Tequila Ocho la Estancia, lime, spinach cordial, lemon ginger mousse and celery bitters.

23 rue Mazarine, 6th
prescriptioncocktailclub.com
@prescriptioncocktailclubparis
⊘ 🗎

Maison Verot

Calling all cured meat lovers, a visit to superstar Gilles Verot's shop is a must. As a third generation *charcutier*, he is renowned for his *pâté en croute*, *terrines*, *rillettes* and *saucissons* using only quality sourced products. He sources milled organic flour for the *croûtes* and pastry crust, and meats from breeders who also share a mutual respect for the animal. Michelin-starred chefs such as Daniel Boulud in NYC are long-time fans of his work. 'Work' meaning *de la tête au pied* – the responsible act of using the entire animal 'from nose to tail', not wasting an ounce of the animal's body. You'll find everything from dry-cured sausage, *andouille* head cheese, *duck à l'orange en croûte*, tripe, rabbit *terrines*, *jambon persillé* and more. In January, when most bakeries are doing the *Galettes des Rois* with sugar, butter and praline, his rustic-luxury version is packed with pork and *foie gras*.

3 rue Notre-Dame des Champs, 6th
Other location: 38 rue de Bretagne, 3rd,
for more locations see website
maisonverot.fr
@maison_verot

La Cave des Papilles

La Cave des Papilles

When it comes to purists of natural wine, look no further than this well-known bottle shop, owned by former sommelier Ewen Le Moigne (*Clown Bar, Saturne*). Not only does he bring together serious unicorn bottles from star producers, he also travels extensively to visit *vignerons* to curate his latest carefully sourced discoveries all under one roof. Throughout the year he hosts tastings where regulars and visitors can come in to meet the winemakers and congregate with other like-minded enthusiasts. They also have savoury snacks like cured sausages and olive oils to host your own apéro. Since it's situated on the corner of the incredible food street rue Daguerre, you can find bakeries etc. for dinner to go with a wine purchase. If it's a bit too far, check out their online shop where they feature their latest bottles, available for same-day delivery (rare for Paris).

35 rue Daguerre, 14th
lacavedespapilles.com
@lacavedespapilles

Boulangerie Archibald

For artisanal bakers and sourdough enthusiasts, mass-produced bread made quickly with cheap ingredients is unthinkable. This tight-knit community from all over the world seek out authentic bread and are avid defenders of breads made by hand, using natural yeasts for slow, long-fermentation times, made with ancient grains (like Einkorn) and organic flours that do not contain pesticide residues or other harmful chemicals. If that speaks to you, head direct to *Archibald* bakery. The aromas, crispy outer crust and soft crumb from the fresh bread speak for themselves. In each of their four locations, the products are sold by weight, in pieces or by the slice, straight from the oven. In addition to the top-quality bread, you'll find savoury crackers, focaccia, seasonal fruit tarts, sugared brioche and even granola.

28 rue des Fossés Saint-Bernard, 5th
Other locations: 15th, 16th, 17th
archibald.bio
@boulangerie.archibald

Fromager Laurent Dubois

Award-winning cheesemonger Laurent Dubois' shop is a work of art – shelves are heaving with hundreds of raw-milk cheeses aged on site in his underground caves. He comes from a family of cheesemakers and travels to small farms regularly to meet artisans who care for the animals' diet, good health and careful production of cheese. The shop is organised with cheeses presented from mild to strong and creamy to hard with goat's, sheep's and cow's milk. He has a keen eye and creative touch too, pairing creamy Brie layered with walnut, or a sharp hard sheep's milk with black truffle or a tangy goat's cheese topped with confit lemon and crushed timut pepper, which has citrus notes. It can seem overwhelming at first, but the friendly and super-knowledgeable staff can guide you, as well as vacuum seal your favourites to take home with you (that passes TSA airport security guidelines).

47 ter blvd Saint-Germain, 6th
Other locations: 4th, 5th, 15th,
fromageslaurentdubois.fr
@laurentdubois_fromager_paris

Olga Vins et Fromages

It was a genius move when Camille Fourmont, owner of the wildly popular La Buvette natural wine bar in the 11th, recently opened *Olga* sandwich-cheese-wine shop in an otherwise non-descript neighbourhood next to the Gare du Lyon train station. Since the area is mostly residential on the perimeter of a massive transportation hub, it hadn't been a destination for food and wine until she took over this vintage chocolate shop – the pretty mirrored décor still intact. Locals have a place to shop or watch the world go by with food served on ceramic plates that she made. Camille is also a local hero to those that travel southbound. Long gone are the days of dreadful train food for long distances that beg for a proper to-go picnic. Choose from juicy bottles of wine, paired with crunchy baguettes filled with three simple seasonal ingredients like homemade apple butter, pesto or green tomato jam, layered with pickled cherries or carrots and goat's or blue cheese. For apéro, you'll need bite-sized snacks like her famous 'buvette' white beans.

3 rue Michel Chasles, 12th
@olga_vins_et_fromages

Olga Vins et Fromages

Muséum National d'Histoire Naturelle

When the weather isn't cooperating, you could spend the entire day (if not weeks) at this collection of five galleries inside the Jardins des Plantes, dubbed the 'Louvre of Natural Science'. The Gallery of Evolution is sure to please everyone from kids to adults with its massive central hall devoted to life-size animals that have disappeared or are in danger of extinction. The Gallery of Mineralogy has over 600,000 stones and fossils, The Gallery of Botany's collection represents 7.5 million plants and The Gallery of Paleontology and Comparative Anatomy features gigantic dinosaur and mammoth skeletons. Outside in the Jardin des Plantes you'll find greenhouse keeping tropical plants at a steady temperature of 22 degrees Celsius while the Ménagerie is the second-oldest public zoo in the world, housing more than 600 mammals, birds, reptiles and amphibians.

57 rue Cuvier, 5th
mnhn.fr
@le_museum

Les Pavillons de Bercy

Just beyond the gates of the old stone wine storage cellars of Bercy, you'll find one of the most unusual museums centred around the curiosities of 19th- and 20th-century fun fairs, called the Museum of Fairground Arts. It's like stepping back in time, playing with carefully restored century-old rides and attractions from the Belle Époque era, when onlookers would crowd into mechanical theatres, cinemas and wax museums to see scientific demonstrations – when bicycles were rare objects. Not only will you see 14 rides, such as a wooden horse carousel, but many are presented using the latest technology in sound and video projection. It is open to the public, but only reservations in advance are led by a speaker or a magician.

53 av des Terroirs-de-France, 12th
arts-forains.com
☺

Accor Arena

The Paris-Bercy, or *Accor Arena*, is an indoor sports arena and concert hall that can seat up to 20,000 people. Throughout the year it hosts sold-out tournaments for major tennis, martial arts, boxing, track cycling, gymnastic and NBA events. It was here that the Chicago Bulls beat the Detroit Pistons 126–108 on 19 January 2023. As a state-of-the-art music venue, it has hosted everyone from Johnny Hallyday to Céline Dion, Daft Punk, Pink Floyd, Madonna and more. Advance programming and tickets are available on their website with pricing for individuals or VIP private boxes for special groups.

8 blvd de Bercy, 12th
accorarena.com
@accor_arena

Bibliothèque Mazarine

The visitors taking photos on the pedestrian Pont des Arts bridge linking the Louvre's right bank entrance to left bank St Germain are blissfully unaware that the gold dome in their photos houses the most beautiful and oldest public library in France. Whether you are a student, teacher, researcher or curious tourist, you shouldn't pass up the chance to see the *Bibliothèque Mazarine*. Founded in the 17th century, it houses over 600,000 volumes, including French history from the 12th to 17th centuries and rare, Medieval manuscripts. Its highlight is a 13th-century Gutenberg Bible (also known as the Mazarine Bible) in a secured vault with a replica on display in the main reading room for everyone to see. With a quick free registration at the desk for day-passes, you can access this incredible historic institution, modernized with wi-fi and charging plugs.

23 quai de Conti, 6th
bibliotheque-mazarine.fr/en/
@labibliothequemazarine
⊛

Musée de Cluny

Sitting on the busy Blvd St Germain, most visitors miss the fantastic Cluny Museum, simply because the flamboyant Gothic façade is out of view on the back side of the boulevard, opposite the Sorbonne. Officially called the National Museum of the Middle Ages, it originally housed the abbots of the order of Cluny in Burgundy in the 13th century. Today, it is a museum devoted to furniture, sculpture, stained glass windows and works of art like goldsmithing and tapestries from Antiquity, the Middle Ages and the Renaissance. High points are the vast vaulted Gallo-Roman thermal baths of Cluny, among the best preserved in the north of France, and the 'Lady and the Unicorn' tapestry. For gardeners and foodies, don't miss the Medieval-inspired food garden outdoors, on the Blvd St Germain side, with seasonal herbs and produce grown all year around.

28 rue du Sommerard, 5th
musee-moyenage.fr
@museecluny

East

The eastern edge of Paris is most identified with the trendy 11th, but there is also more to visit in the 19th and 20th where a multicultural mix of young people and an older generation of Parisian families co-exist, live, eat and play. From the Bastille monument north of the Canal Saint Martin and Parc de la Villette, eastern Paris' main arteries in the 11th's rue Oberkampf, rue Saint-Maur and rue de Charonne will appeal to culinary enthusiasts for family-owned shops, food markets, bakeries, craft coffee shops, wine bars, cool restaurants and lively nightlife vibe. The Belleville neighbourhood in the 19th is notable for its street art, international restaurants, cocktail bars and funky nightlife scene. If you need a break from pulsing energy, head to one of the immense green parks, boat canals and renowned cultural institutions in the 19th, like the Parc de la Villette, with its group of museums including the Cité des Sciences, Cité de la Musique, and the spectacular Philharmonie de Paris – or head to the 20th, home to the world's most visited cemetery, Père Lachaise, the final resting place of the rich and infamous.

Le Cadoret

One of the joys of this friendly brother and sister-owned neighbourhood spot is in finding it. Food travellers, chefs and winemakers from all over the world come to eat and drink at Louis and Léa's relaxed café and bistrot in Belleville. Expect to see Louis holding court behind the vintage zinc bar, chatting with customers while making espresso or pouring natural wines, whilst Léa's home cooking brings regulars back more than once a week for the affordable set *prix fixe* lunches and/or the *à la carte* dinners. As an all-day café you can enjoy coffee and a pastry at the bar in the morning, have lunch or dinner on the likes of suckling pig with puréed potatoes or delicate *lieu jaune* (pollack) with *beurre blanc* butter, and in-between it is the perfect spot for apéro drinks and nibbles with locals and Lou at the bar.

1 rue Pradier, 19th
@le_cadoret
⊘ (bar) 🍽 (bistrot)

Septime

Although this sustainable, internationally recognized restaurant is a challenging reservation, due to over demand for one of its limited seats, it is still the same humble neighbourhood spot since opening in 2011. It is an important period to note as this is when many Parisian chefs were noticing a collective shift away from pretentious formal restaurants towards a more relaxed, approachable way of dining out. Friends turned business partners Bertrand Grébaut (formerly of Alain Passard's three-star *L'Arpège*) and Théo Pourriat took notice, and the rest is history. It's hard to imagine today, but kitchens that opened directly onto no-frills dining rooms and a kitchen brigade informally bringing plates to the table were unheard of. Expect welcoming service in an intimate setting and sophisticated set tasting menus paired with natural wines. *Septime* accepts reservations three weeks in advance. Next door, Septime La Cave, a wine bar, and seafood-focused Clamato, are walk-in only.

80 rue de Charonne, 11th
@septimeparis
septime-charonne.fr
⊘ 🗓 (three weeks in advance)

Bistrot Paul Bert

Even after nearly three decades, Bertrand Auboyneau's 'BPB' is still one of the most sought-after bistrot experiences in the world. Regulars and first-time visitors book weeks in advance for a table in one of the two distinctly different rooms, either the intimate right side with white tablecloths or the buzzy left side with bare wooden tables. The daily changing menu is a masterclass in seasonal French comfort food, most notably the classic peppercorn *filet-frites*. In winter, you'll find plenty of butter, cream, truffles and *foie gras* and nose-to-tail cooking with offal such as bone marrow, sweetbreads, kidneys, brains, etc. In spring and summer, their garden provides bright green asparagus, artichokes, courgette blossoms, tomatoes, berries and cherries. The portions are hearty and generous, so if you can manage dessert, the Paris-Brest praline cream pastry (in winter) is a must and the Grand Marnier soufflés are made to order, but worth the wait.

18 rue Paul Bert, 11th
@bistrotpaulbert

Maison Sota

Rainy days are built for relaxed long meals particularly at Sota Atsumi's *Maison Sota*, with its chic and refined tasting menus. Having first made his name at the wildly popular Clown Bar, Sota's dream was always to create a restaurant experience where each person has a view onto the open kitchen, cooking intimately for them as if they were in his home. Although the atmosphere is relaxed, ascending the grand staircase from the main foyer up to the mezzanine dining room is *pure* glamour. Expect to see and be seen as you reach the top, greeted by the expansive professional kitchen with a roaring wood-burning oven and buzzy open-plan dining room. His menus change each day with fresh seasonal ingredients walked in the door by the farmers, fishermen and hunters, paired with both classic and natural wines. Anticipate beautifully presented, delicious dishes such as wild venison with persimmon, oyster, chestnut and apple caramel, dressed in walnut-black pepper meat *jus*.

3 rue Saint-Hubert, 11th
@maison_sota
maison-sota.com

Le Cheval d'Or

The Golden Horse is a former 80s Chinese eatery in Belleville, now an exciting Asian-fusion bistrot with a fiercely loyal fan base. Its vintage façade remains, but inside the expansive narrow room is modern and bright with white-washed walls, an eating counter in front of a bustling open kitchen and a beautiful, seated dining room just beyond a tall, elegant archway. Highlights of the à la carte menu are the decadent *croque madame* sandwich loaded with shrimp, lobster, fried egg, chilli oil and mayonnaise; the steamed scallops with XO sauce and crispy vermicelli; pork agnolotti ravioli with tofu mayo, shiitake and ricotta, and stuffed Peking duck with crêpes, rice and house hoisin sauce. For dessert, expect classic and modern like the *Île flottante* with corn cream and caramelized popcorn. The friendly somms are passionate about their natural wine list and eager to make suggestions for you.

21 rue de la Villette, 19th
@chevaldorparis
chevaldorparis.com

Combat

Wedged between dim sum, Thai and wonton ravioli shops, *Combat* cocktail bar is at the heart of the nightlife scene on the bustling rue de Belleville. You can't miss the mustard-yellow tiles behind the bar, greenery hanging from the ceiling nor the neon bathroom – but it's the exceptional bar talent, great food and drink and devoted crowd that speak volumes about the place. You'll find everyone from hip-hop music execs to creatives wearing suits, sneakers, scooter helmets and baseball hats – everyone is welcome. The affordable cocktail list changes often, with *cocktails du jour* like rum, pistachio, Stracciatella, gum liqueur and orange blossom, or tequila, capers, gentian, walnuts, white vermouth and lime.

63 rue de Belleville, 19th
@combat.belleville
⊘

Bar Principal

This cocktail-natural wine bar is packed every day of the week, rain or shine. In this mostly local, family-centric neighbourhood you'll see a real slice of Parisian life, with kids playing ball in the street, dog happy-hour meet-ups and 20-somethings catching up after work on the small, covered terrace. Open until late night, the mid-century candlelit interior is a favourite rendezvous spot – featuring six classic cocktails that change every week, like the clever Kevin Bacon: an orange wine reduction with whisky-infused bacon, tomato and sage, or the savoury *Bendito*: a pisco-infused palo santo, sake, with fino and lemon. The bar food is anything but boring with the juicy fried chicken, grilled *croque monsieur* sandwich with aged Comté cheese and black trumpet mushrooms, or the juicy 'non-smashed burger' with smoked paprika mayo. Not a cocktail person? They've got you with natural wines and craft beer.

5 rue du Général Renault, 11th
@barprincipalparis
⊘

Bar Principal

Aux Deux Amis

David Loyola's retro bar on the rue Oberkampf is something of
a local legend, a humble neighbourhood no-frills gathering spot,
bringing together a community of animated regulars and other
international wine-bar friends. This is a straightforward place
where what you see is what you get with short concise menu
options written in chalk pen on the window or bar mirror. Lunch
is a calm affair, compared to the raucous late-night after-dinner
vibe. Start with a little plate of charcuterie and hazelnuts, before
blue cheese endive salad, braised beef cheeks, juicy duck breast
with buttery whipped potatoes or clams with Bellota chorizo.
Don't let the crowd that seems to know each other deter you –
once inside, the sociable staff will help you fit right in and can
walk you through the affordable wine lists and tapas options.

45 rue Oberkampf, 11th
@auxdeuxamis